SOUS VIDE COOKBOOK FOR BEGINNERS 2021

BEST RECIPES OFALL TIME

TABLE OF CONTENTS

INTRODUCTION

Sous vide (pronounced *sue-veed*) is a cooking technique that utilizes precise temperature control to deliver consistent, restaurant-quality results. High-end restaurants have been using sous vide cooking for years to cook food to the exact level of doneness desired, every time. The technique recently became popular for home cooks with the availability of affordable and easy-to-use sous vide precision cooking equipment.

Sous vide, which means *"under vacuum"* in French, refers to the process of vacuum-sealing food in a bag, then cooking it to a very precise temperature in a water bath. This technique produces results that are impossible to achieve through any other cooking method.

Sous vide cooking is much easier than you might think, and usually involved three simple steps:

. Attach your precision cooker to a pot of water and set the time and temperature according to your desired level of doneness.

2. Put your food in a sealable bag and clip it to the side of the pot.

3. Finish by searing, grilling, or broiling the food to add a crispy, golden exterior layer.

Why should I cook sous vide?

Sous vide cooking uses exact temperature control with circulation to produce results that you can't achieve through any other cooking technique. The reason is that, when using traditional methods of cooking, you don't have control over heat and temperature. Consequently, it's very difficult and time consuming to consistently cook great food. Food ends up overcooked on the outside, with only a small portion in the center that is cooked to the temperature you want. Food loses flavor, overcooks easily, and ends up with a dry, chewy texture.

With precise temperature control in the kitchen, sous vide provides the following benefits:

Consistency: Because you cook your food to a precise temperature for a precise amount of time, you can expect very consistent results.

Taste: Food cooks in its juices. This ensures that the food is moist, juicy and tender.

Waste reduction: Traditionally prepared food dries out and results in waste. For example, on average, traditionally cooked steak loses up to 40% of its volume due to drying out. Steak cooked via precision cooking, loses none of its volume.

Flexibility: Traditional cooking can require your constant attention. Precision cooking brings food to an exact temperature and holds it. There is no worry about overcooking.

How Are Sous Vide Results Better?

Sous vide provides down-to-the-degree control in the kitchen to deliver the most tender, flavorful food you've ever had. With Anova, it's super simple to get restaurant-quality results from edge to edge.

Sous Vide Steak vs. Traditionally Cooked Steak

The steak on the left was cooked sous vide at 129ºF, while the steak on the right was pan-cooked. As illustrated in the comparison above between cooking sous vide steak and pan-cooking steak, there are important advantages to cooking sous vide over traditional methods.

Sous Vide Salmon vs. Traditionally Cooked Salmon

The salmon cooked with Anova (left) remains a translucent pink, with a delicate, flaky texture. The pan-cooked salmon (right) has overcooked edges because the surface temperature of the pan is higher than the target cooking temperature. As it dries out, it begins to expel the white albumin.

Sous Vide Eggs vs. Traditionally Cooked Eggs

Whether you're a poached egg perfectionist or a fan of soft-boiled, sous vide makes your ideal egg achievable every time. The egg on the leftcooked consistently to the desired texture. On the right, a guessing game resulted in raw and runny yolks with over-thickened whites.

What Equipment Do I Need To Cook Sous Vide?

It's actually very affordable and easy to get started with sous vide cooking thanks to the recent availability of sous vide devices built for the home cook. You'll need a few things:

- A sous vide precision cooking device

- Packaging for your food, like resealable bags or canning jars

- A container to hold the water

Types of Sous Vide Machines

Sous vide equipment has existed for decades in professional kitchens around the world, but it has always been bulky, expensive, and overloaded with complex features. This type of equipment eventually made its way into high-end specialty retail shops but remained limited to chefs and consumers with extensive culinary experience.

Cooking shows, social media, and online communities have furthered consumers' knowledge of sous vide cooking, but it wasn't until Anova released the first affordable and easy-to-use consumer device that sous vide became accessible to home cooks. There are now many sous vide options available to the home cook.

Below are a few types of equipment for you to consider when you're ready to build your ultimate sous vide setup:

Sous Vide Immersion Circulator

The Anova Precision® Cooker is a standalone immersion circulator that heats water and circulates it around the pot to maintain precise temperatures evenly. Immersion circulators are an affordable and easy-to-use sous vide machine option. They do not come with a built-in water bath, so they take up very little space in your kitchen. Standalone sous vide devices don't require additional equipment to get started because they clamp on and adjust to any pot you already own. The Anova Precision® Cooker is a sous vide immersion circulator. Other examples include Chef Steps Joule, Nomiku, and Sansaire.

Sous Vide Water Oven

Water ovens are often referred to as countertop water baths. They are fully-contained, sous vide devices that are about the size of a microwave and typically cost $500+. Sous vide water ovens heat water, but unlike immersion circulators, they do not circulate the water. This can lead to inconsistencies in the food's resulting texture. Examples of water ovens include SousVide Supreme, AquaChef, and Gourmia. Multi-use cookers like Oliso, Gourmia and Instant Pot also offer sous vide appliances.

DIY Sous Vide Hacks

Cooler, rice cooker, and slow cooker hacks are great options for exploring sous vide cooking before you decide to purchase a device. The Food Lab's J. Kenji Lopez-Alt has a great post on sous vide beer cooler hacks.

Sous Vide Packaging

Sealing foods prevents evaporation and allows for the most efficient transfer energy from the water to the food. To do so, simply place your seasoned food in a plastic bag and remove the air using the water immersion technique, a straw, or a vacuum sealer.

You don't need a vacuum sealer to cook sous vide. There are lots of options, here are a few of the best types of sous vide packaging:

Resealable Bags or Jars

Resealable bags are very versatile, and can be used with the water immersion method to remove air from the bag. We recommend heavy-duty, BPA-free bags, like Ziplock's freezer bags.

Reusable Silicone Bags

Reusable sous vide bags made from silicone, like these Stasher Reusable Silicone Sous Vide Bag bags, make it easy to enjoy they same quality results night after night.

Vacuum Sealing Bags

You don't need to purchase a vacuum sealer and vacuum seal bags, but they work well for batch cooking. Foodsaver and Oliso are great options, and both are pretty affordable.

Canning Jars

Several different types of foods can also be cooked in glass canning jars. Beans and grains both work well in jars, as do desserts such as cakes and custards. Get tips on cooking sous vide with jars in our Guide to Sous Vide Cooking with Canning Jars.

Sous Vide Containers

Anova clips onto the side of any pot or vessel with an adjustable clamp. So, you can use any size of pot that you already have at home. If you're planning to cook a lot of food at once, plastic bins like Cambro and Rubbermaid are great choices.

You can also explore creating a dedicated sous vide cooking vessel. Our community members have created some crafty cooler and cambro hacks. Take a look at this guide on the best sous vide containers.

BRIEF HISTORY OF SOUS VIDE

When sous vide arrived in the food world, the technique wasn't initially used to make food taste better. In the late 1960s, when food-grade plastic films and vacuum packing were mastered by French and American engineers, sous vide was used as a safety measure: The ability to keep packaged foods in a water bath at a certain temperature made pasteurizing and sterilizing easier for labs, hospitals, and large-scale commercial food companies. Originally, vacuum packing and cooking foods sous vide was used to seal and pasteurize industrially prepared foods so that they would have a longer shelf life.

But then in 1974, sous vide made its way into the restaurant scene. (Well, kind of.) French chef Pierre Troisgros wanted to develop a new way to cook foie gras, and he hired Georges Pralus, another chef, to help. The goal? To lose as little fat as possible when cooking. After all, fat is flavor, and foie gras is all about fatty flavor. Through experimentation, Pralus found that the liver lost the least amount of fat when poached at a precise temperature, sealed in plastic.

Around the same time, Bruno Goussault—an economist, inventor, and chef —made similar discoveries for commercial food operations and hospitals. In the 1980s, he teamed up with Chef Joël Robuchon to create a sous vide dining program for the French railroad. This paved the way for Goussault's next career move: He has been the chief scientist at Cuisine Solutions, an American company that specializes in sous vide food preparation and packaging, since 1989.

The technique slowly spread to chefs in the U.S.— largely thanks to the Internet. Chefs began to acquire sous vide circulators for their kitchens in the early 2000s. (Thomas Keller was one of the first.) The only problem: No one really knew how to use them. None of these chefs had come up in the kitchen world using them. No one had spent time experimenting with them. Enter: the website eGullet. The forums on this culinary-minded site were a place for people to geek out on food-related issues, and sous vide was a perfect subject.

Cutting-edge chefs like Chicago's Grant Achatz, Charleston's Sean Brock, and New York's Wylie Dufresne, and many others would talk about what they were playing with, and how they used different times and temperatures for different proteins.

In 2005, sous vide started to really pickup. Joan Roca, a chef in Spain, wrote a book about sous vide that arrived in the U.S. that year (with a slightly rocky translation). Chef Grant Achatz's restaurant, Alinea, also opened—sous vide circulators included. Chef and inventor Dave Arnold began to teach low-temperature cooking classes at the French Culinary Institute.

"Cryovacking, which is more often called sous vide (French for "under vacuum"), is poised to change the way restaurant chefs cook," wrote Amanda Hesser for the New York Times in a 2005 story called "Under Pressure." "And like the Wolf stove and the immersion blender, it will probably trickle down to the home kitchen someday."

In 2006, Dufresne battled Mario Batali on Iron Chef America; it was the first time sous vide circulators were seen on TV. The demand only grew from there.

The move into home kitchens has also been slow, and largely due to the influx of sous vide circulators with a lower price point, as professional devices cost over $1,000. In 2009, Sous Vide Supreme debuted as the first circulator for less than $500. In 2012, another sous vide circulator company called Nomiku launched, and they started selling machines for $359. In 2016, ChefSteps released their own circulator, called the Joule, for just $199. (In 2017, we named the Joule our top pick for the home cook.)

SOUS VIDE COOKING: GETTING STARTED

In the recent days, you have probably been caught in the hype of sous-vide cooking. I know you are also tempted to join this revolutionary movement. This is especially so because we realize that you can cook a healthy meal without overcooking or burning it.

The cooking process can really confuse you as a beginner but worry not because its something you can quickly learn.

Whether you are green in the field or have some basic information, you need to follow a guide for perfection. You will only find the guide in a good sous vide cookbook.

Unfortunately, just like sous vide cooking has taken the world by storm, there are thousand of sous vide cookbooks in the market all with varying information.

For this reason, it's hard to choose a book that will help you. This article will guide you in choosing the best cookbook.

WHAT IS SOUS VIDE COOKING?

Sous vide cooking has been around for quite some time. According to Wikipedia, it was first mentioned by Sir Benjamin Thompson in 1799. Yet, only in recent years has it started going mainstream and into home kitchens. This is all thanks to the so called 'modernist' cooking movement. While the name 'sous vide' sounds pretty fancy, it's really simple in practice. Simpler than most people would imagine.

This method of cooking does take a bit longer than traditional methods, but it yields results that are practically impossible to achieve otherwise. It allows cooking food at a much lower and precisely controlled temperature. Many people find this makes meats more tender and vegetables better-flavored. This is because the food is cooked evenly throughout, keeping the juices and the aroma inside.

Putting it simply, sous vide is a cooking method where meat or vegetables are tightly sealed in a plastic bag and placed in a water bath that maintains a specific temperature. With this method, the food avoids exposure to high temperatures, which helps to avoid overcooking and drying out. This makes sous vide method very useful for cooking fish which is very easy to overcook using traditional methods.

Depending on the food you cook, you may or may not need specialized equipment such as a sous vide immersion circulator. Different foods require different degrees of accuracy and constancy of cooking temperature. Salmon fillets generally need about 40 to 60 minutes depending on size and thickness. As such, a common boiling pot and an instant-read thermometer is all that will suffice with a little tending.

You must have heard people use the term in the high-end restaurants or during cooking competitions. That's because those restaurants have used the cooking method for ages before people started using it at home.

The phrase is a French term that means 'under the vacuum' which is exactly what happens in this method of cooking. The chef marinates their proteins then vacuum seals it and put it in a pot of water. this means that the food never comes to contact with flames and heated metal surface.

The machine heats the water to a constant high but not boiling point level. Yet it also maintains the temperature never fluctuating between high and low. It's simply like you are cooking in a controlled water bath.

You can cook almost anything with this method of cooking from eggs, meat, fish or seafood the list is endless. What's more, the result is unparalleled because it cooks way better than the traditional method of cooking.

WHY SHOULD YOU COOK SOUS VIDE?

This method of cooking gives you a controlled temperature making your food slow cook within a set time. You get consistent results from a consistent method of cooking.

The food retains its taste because it cooks in its juice. You develop a juicy moist and tender dish.

The traditional method of cooking results in waste from drying out.

A good example is, when grilling a steak, it loses some percentage of the meat because it dries out. Sous vide cooking retains the same volume of meat.

When you are cooking traditionally you must constantly check the food to confirm that it reaches the desired consistency. When it comes to sous vide you don't need to protect the food from overcooking. You just set the temperature and time the meal takes to cook then go check it when the time lapses.

It lets you focus on other roles as you cook in the sous vide. Because it will take the set time you set it to and you don't have to worry about overcooking.

Like earlier stated, the results you get with a traditional cooking method is nothing like the sous vide cooking. It cooks your meats from edge to edge and from center to the outer part.

SOUS VIDE COOKING TECHNIQUE

This culinary technique cuts beyond fashion to offer you a professional meal that is not only succulent but well done too. It's like poaching your food in a vacuum bag under a specific temperature. The machine has water that retains a steady temperature while circulating and ultimately cooking.

This circulation helps to maintain the temperature. The method suits those who want to limit the amount of fat/oil they use in food. You don't need to add fat or oil, especially in the proteins because the food will cook in its juices.

This will leave your food not only rich in flavor but also soft, juicy and moist. Note that, if you love searing your meats you won't do it before placing the meat in the sous vide. Rather you can do it once its cooked.

WHICH ARE THE BEST MEALS TO COOK IN A SOUS VIDE

Sous vide cooking is versatile in that it allows you to cook a wide range of proteins and veggies. Most people think its good for cooking meats only but that isn't true.

Since the technique ensures overcooking is off the window you can use it to cook meals that tend to overcook or dry out. This includes steak, pork chops, seafood, duck breasts, turkey and chicken breasts.

If your meat has lots of connective tissues use this method. Some of these meats with connective tissues include chicken feet, oxtail, and the beef tongue.

Except for those times when you want to fry your eggs, you can use it to cook scrambled eggs, poach the egg, make an eggnog or pasteurize it to use in your raw cookie dough.

The best part is that you can use it even for your veggies. I know this is a surprise to many but veggies like carrots or asparagus will wow you if you sous vide specific recipes.

You can use your sous vide even for deserts. All those desserts that you cook in a Bain Marie will work perfectly when cooked using this technique. Consider cooking pumpkin pie, cream brulee or cheesecake using this method. Also, make the ham and delicious burgers.

Other meals you can use this method to cook include mashed potatoes, beef stock and puree which I love and it took a friend to convince me to prepare it using this method. It wowed me and I'm sure it will wow you.

HOW TO SOUS VIDE

We will try to break it down in a few steps to make it easy to understand.

- *Step 1: There are equipment's you need for the whole cooking process.*

The first one is a sous vide cooking equipment which was initially utterly expensive but today you can even improvise if you have a sous vide precision cooking machine, a large pot to hold water and a vacuum seal bag.

- ### *Step 2: The preparation of the meat*

By preparation, we are referring to the seasoning process or marination. Seasoning part will determine the flavors of your meat. When cooking sous vide you can decide to use only salt and pepper. But, if you want to add a little more flavors, feel free to play around with your spices.

When cooking meat, I often use ground black pepper, curry, ginger, soy sauce, and harissa paste. You can use almost anything you want. With this process, you can have a dish full of flavor because the seasoning gets absorbed within the meat making it flavorful.

- ### *Step 2: Vacuum Sealing*

You have the vacuum seal bag, right?

Immediately after the marination, place it in a vacuum seal bag. For safety, choose a gold standard food grade vacuum seal bag or the normal resealable freezer bag. Before you seal it consider adding aromatics like bay leaves or rosemary for a sweet aroma.

Let the leaves remain in contact with the meat before you seal. If you desire, add some ghee or butter but avoid liquids that deter the flavor sealing process.

Go ahead and follow the manufacturer's instruction for the proper sealing. If possible seal it two to three times to ensure it stays sealed.

- ### *Step 3: Temperature setting*

The good thing about a sous vide is that it gives you the pinpoint temperature set to choose. But before that, fill your large pot with water then set the temperature depending on what you are cooking.

I always use the given temperature ranges just to be sure. You see, it depends on whether you want your meat rare, medium-cooked or fully-cooked. A good example is that the medium-rare meat temperature ranges between 130°F TO 139°F.

If you will set your sous vide machine at this temperature, you will have a medium-rare meat. The setting temperature part may confuse you but when you have good brands this won't be an issue.

The brands have software to determine the correct temperature to cook your food if you key in the details on the app. Once you set the temperature and the water reaches the set temperature, place the vacuum sealed bag in the water and let it circulate around.

Note that, some bags need you to pin at the side of the pot just to be sure that the seal doesn't fail.

- ***Step 4: Decide how long the food should sous vide***

You need to know how long the food should take to sous vide. This is because the cooking process involves heat the food, tenderizing then make sure it's safe.

It may take between 1 to 2 hours for the meat to heat up entirely.

The tenderizing process determines whether your meat will be chewy, fatty or fully cooked. If you have a big chunk of meat you may want to tenderize it for up to 2 days. However, some meat parts will take 2-24 hours just know the kind of meat you are prepping.

For the food safety, remember to keep the food at 40°F and 134°F for a short duration otherwise your food safety becomes risky. Take anything less than 4 hours at such temperature.

- ***Step 5: Finish***

Remove your meats or other thing being cooked from the water and let it rest for between 10-20 minutes. Go ahead and serve or if you need to sear, it remove the meat from the bag and dry it with your kitchen towel.

In a hot skillet, sear it on both sides to form the crust you need.

THE WORST & BEST FOODS TO COOK SOUS VIDE

One of the great things about sous vide cooking is that you can use the technique to cook more or less anything.

Experimenting with different foods to see how they taste when cooked sous vide is half of the fun, and you can't go far wrong with using most ingredients, but there are some foods which definitely work better when cooked sous vide than others, which we're going to take a quick look at here.

THE BEST FOODS TO COOK SOUS VIDE

- ***Tougher Cuts Of Meat***

What's important to remember here is that a 'tougher' or 'cheaper' cut of meat, doesn't necessarily mean a 'worse' cut.

The reason that cuts such as the neck and leg are cheaper and less desirable is that they are constantly in motion on the animal, meaning that the protein strands in the muscles are much more robust, making them tougher to cook and eat, and hence, cheaper to buy from the butcher.

But this is where your sous vide machine comes in! The sous vide process breaks down these tough proteins and gives you a super tender cut, all from a product which most people would discard.

Usually braised like pulled pork, when it's cooked using sous vide it can actually become more like a tender steak. Delicious!

- ### *Eggs*

Eggs are one of the most popular foods to cook sous-vide for a couple of reasons. The most obvious is the control over texture that the method gives.

Because of the precise control of sous vide, you can control the exact consistency of your egg, so be sure to check out our guide to a perfect sous vide egg to determine how long you need to leave yours for, and at what temperature, from 'flowing cream' to 'pliable camembert.' Starbucks recent made sous vide eggs famous with their 'sous vide egg bites.'

Once you've got that consistency nailed, sous vide allows you to cook, consistently, eggs to perfection each and every time.

The second reason chefs love sous vide eggs so much is because of how easy it is to do! Due to the fact that the eggs are already contained within their shells, there's no need for them to be vacuum packed.

- ### *Pork*

Pork often has a bit of reputation as being one of the blander, drier meats. However, it's a prime example of the wonders of sous vide.

The problem is that conventional cooking methods lose a lot of the fats and juices of pork, but sous vide retains these fats, turning them into flavour.

As an example, take a look at our recipe for how to cook pork rack sous-vide.

- *Lamb*

Lamb is another meat which is difficult to get right, with many cooks overdoing it, resulting in chewy, tough meat, and others overcompensating too much and leaving it undercooked.

This all means that it's great for sous vide, removing all of the guesswork and guaranteeing a succulent, flavourful cut which you don't have to constantly keep your eye on.

If you've always viewed lamb as a little bit boring, try it sous vide, such as in our recipe for lamb rump sous vide.

- *Carrots*

Vegetables are, by and large great for cooking sous vide, keeping them firm and crisp, and sous vide carrots are particularly good.

What's great is that not only do you achieve the perfect texture, you can also infuse the carrots with things such as herbs and duck fat, all of which will infuse with the carrot to take it to the next level, before browning the carrots afterwards to caramelise their natural sugars.

THE WORST FOODS TO COOK SOUS VIDE

- *Filleted Fish*

While you certainly can cook fish sous vide, depending on your personal preferences, you might not want to.

The problem is that a filleted fish is simply too delicate and flaky to cook in sous-vide machine, and once it's gone through the process, it'll simply fall apart as you try to get it out of the bag.

Perhaps if you'd like to try out some sous vide seafood, you should try shellfish, like these tasty sous vide scallops.

- *Liver*

There are some foods which feasibly can be cooked via sous vide, but simply aren't worth the time, and liver is one of those foods.

Liver is such a lean product to begin with, that it really doesn't benefit enough from the effects of sous vide, and you're probably best off simply cooking it in the pan instead.

- *Fillet Steak*

This might be a controversial one with some, and it might be a bit harsh to term it "one of the worst" foods to cook sous vide, but Chris believes that sous vide is somewhat wasted on a cut of fillet steak.

This is for a similar reason to those outlined with liver, and it's just that fillet steak is already so tender, that putting in a sous vide machine won't have enough of impact on it.

This isn't to say that you shouldn't cook your steak sous vide, just that the benefits may not be worth the time!

- *Hollandaise*

Hollandaise is notoriously tricky to get right, and while some chefs claim that sous vide makes it fool-proof, this isn't the case.

Sous vide Hollandaise involves mixing egg yolk, lemon juice and butter in your sous vide machine, shaking a few times in the process.

Unfortunately, it's still just as difficult to get right as it would be and just as prone to falling apart and winding up lumpy and unappetising.

INCREDIBLE SOUS VIDE RECIPES

When preparing sous vide recipes, take a few small steps to make this cooking method more Bulletproof. Sous vide cooking traditionally inv olves sealing food in an airtight plastic bag before immersing it in the cooking water. While convenient, this method can cause hormone-disrupting BPA and other harmful compounds to leach into your food.

You can still make incredible sous vide recipes without the plastic: Depending on the recipe, swap the bags with mason jars or reusable silicone bags to keep your food safe and reap the benefits of this gentle cooking method. Sous vide cooking still poses risks for producing histamines, so see how you feel after eating food prepared this way.

From eggs to seafood and desserts, make these sous vide recipes and become the star chef in your kitchen:

BREAKFAST SOUS VIDE RECIPES

- ### <u>SOUS VIDE EGGS</u>

No bags or jars needed: This sous vide recipe creates perfectly slow-poached eggs by cooking them straight in the water bath. With golden runny yolks and just-set whites, these eggs are worth the wait.

What to put your poached eggs on: mashed potatoes, miso buttered toast, bacon and egg breakfast ramen, kimchi stew, crispy bolognese rice bowl, or, you know, everything. Oh, if you don't have a sous vide machine (you should put one on your wishlist!), you can also do slow-poached eggs in a pot too. It takes a bit more hand-holding, but it can be done.

YIELD: Serves 4

ACTIVE TIME: 7 minutes

TOTAL TIME: Overnight, or up to 2 days

Ingredients:

* 1 pound (450g) thick-cut bacon, still in its package (see note)

Instructions:

. Preheat a sous vide water bath to 145°F (63°C). Place bacon, still in its original plastic packaging, directly in water bath and cook for at least 8 and up to 48 hours. When ready to serve, remove from water bath and proceed immediately to step 2, or chill in refrigerator or freezer for later use (see note).

.   To finish, preheat a large skillet or griddle over medium-high heat for 5 minutes. Add bacon and cook, pressing gently with a press or the back of a spatula (just enough to keep it mostly flat), until brown and crisp on the first side, about 2 minutes. Turn bacon and briefly cook on second side, just to remove pale color (about 15 seconds).

3. Transfer to a paper towel-lined plate to remove excess fat. Serve immediately.

- SOUS VIDE SCRAMBLED EGGS

Scrambled eggs are so fast and easy to fry up, and it never occurred to me to cook them in my SousVide Supreme. Who wants to wait twenty minutes for eggs to cook – not to mention the additional time it takes for the water oven to preheat? Not this lazy ass!

YIELD: Serve 2

Ingredients:

- 4 large eggs

- Kosher salt

- Freshly ground black pepper

- 1 tablespoon of butter

- Aleppo pepper (optional)

Instructions:

Fill the water oven with hot water and preheated it to 165 F. In a medium-sized bowl, beat the eggs with a large pinch of salt and four grinds of black pepper.

- Pour the beaten eggs and butter into the silicone bag.

- Using the water displacement method, remove the air from the bag and seal it tight.

- Once the water oven reach 165 F, drop-in the sealed bag.

And set the timer for 10 minutes. After, the buzzer went off, remove the bag from the water and squish it around so the eggs wouldn't form a brick.

Put the bag back in the water and let it cook for 12 more minutes. (In many recipes using plastic bags, the cooking time is only 10 minutes + 6 minutes but since the silicone is thicker, soak the eggs for five more minutes).

- Remove the eggs from the SousVide Supreme.

- Spoon it on a plate, and sprinkle on Aleppo pepper flakes.

- <u>SOUS VIDE EGGS PIZZA</u>

Cook time: 1 hour 20 minutes

Servings: 4

Ingredients:

1. One Pizza Dough

2. Three sous vide eggs

3. Two ounces of fresh mozzarella

4. Three slices of cooked Canadian bacon

5. One tablespoon of Hollandaise sauce

6. Chopped Parsley

7. Two egg yolks

8. Juice from half lemon

9. Salt

10. Cayenne pepper

11. Half a stick of butter

Instructions:

. Combine the egg yolks, lemon, salt, and pepper in a microwave safe bowl and whisk, then add the melted butter before putting in the microwave for fifteen seconds. Then set aside.

For the sous vide eggs:

. Set water bath to 75oC, and drop in the eggs carefully. Cook for fifteen minutes, and then remove after which you put them in cold water to stop the cooking.

For the Pizza:

3. Place a baking tray on the top rack of your oven and pre-heat at 260oC for one hour.

4. Roll out the dough to a 12-inch round and place on a pizza peel lightly dusted with flour.

. Change the oven function to broil. Spread fresh mozzarella and three slices of pre-cooked Canadian bacon on top.

. Place on your baking tray and broil for one minute; afterward, open the oven and rotate pizza 180 degrees. Broil again for another one minute.

. Switch the oven function back and bake for another two minutes before removing from the oven.

. Break the sous vide eggs in a bowl, before placing them on top of the pizza and seasoning with salt and pepper.

9. Carefully drizzle Hollandaise sauce over the eggs with the aid of a spoon and serve.

Chef's tip: The sous vide eggs should be should be 'shocked' to cooling so that the yolks won't completely solidify.

Nutritional information

Calories: 168.7; Fats: 3.6g; Carbohydrates: 8g; Fiber: 1.4g; Protein: 25.5g

BEEF SOUS VIDE RECIPES

- ## <u>SOUS VIDE POT ROAST</u>

Avoid dry, tough cuts of meat with this simple sous vide recipe. Create a quick marinade with rosemary and lemon juice, then immerse your meat and sear to finish. Keep this recipe more Bulletproof and swap soy sauce with coconut aminos, plus avoid eating garlic too often.

Prep time: 15 mins

Cook time: 24 hours

Total time: 24 hours 15 mins

Serves: 6 servings

Ingredients:

- 2 Pound Chuck Roast

- ¼ Cup Lemon Juice

- ¼ Cup Soy Sauce

- 1 teaspoon Minced Garlic

- 1 Sprig Fresh Rosemary

Instructions:

1.   In a Ziplock bag, combine the Lemon Juice, Soy Sauce, Garlic & Rosemary

2.   Place the Roast inside and rub around in the marinade

3.   Seal the bag, removing as much air as possible

.   Place in the Sous Vide Cooker between 130-140* depending on desired doneness (Medium-Rare at 130, Medium-Well at 140).

5.   Cook for 18-24 hours

6.   About halfway through, pull the bag out and rotate the roast in the marinade.

7.   Heat olive oil in a large sauce pan

8.   Sear each side of the roast for about 1 minute

9.   Slice to serve

-       ## SOUS VIDE BEEF FILET TAIL OVER SWEET POTATO MASH

This sous vide recipe takes an already tender cut of beef and transforms it into a buttery starring dish. Meat cooks in the water bath with grass-fed ghee and a zesty paleo dressing before topping a creamy sweet potato or butternut mash. Stay more Bulletproof and get pastured beef, avoid eating garlic and onion too often, and avoid pepper if you are sensitive to nightshades.

Prep Time: 20 mins

Cook Time: 4 hours

Total Time: 4 hours 20 mins

Serves: 2

Ingredients:

Beef Fillet

- 1 Beef Fillet Tail

- 1/4 cup grass fed butter or ghee, softened

- 2 tbs Tessemae's Southwest Ranch

- Sea salt

- Black pepper

- Tallow for searing

Sweet Potato Mash

- 1 large sweet potato, cut into 1-inch cubes

- ¼ cup grass fed butter or ghee divided

- 1 tbs Tessemae's Slow Roasted Garlic Spread

- 1 shallot, diced

- 2 tbs fresh rosemary, chopped

- 1 tbs fresh thyme, chopped

- Sea salt

Instructions:

Beef Fillet

. In a mixing bowl, combine all ingredients except for the beef fillet tail. This will make a compound butter.

. Place compound butter in a vacuum seal bag and then add the beef fillet tail, making sure you coat the beef evenly with the compound butter.

3. Seal the bag and place in a Sous Vide heated to 130 F. Cook for 4 hours.

4. Heat a large cast iron skillet over medium high heat and add about 1 tbs of tallow.

. Once tallow is shimmering, remove beef from Sous Vide and remove from vacuum bag. Pat dry with paper towels.

. Sear beef for about 1-2 minutes per side but no more. This will give a nice crust but won't cook the inside any further.

7. Remove from skillet and let rest for 5-10 minutes.

8. Slice across the grain into medallions and serve over Roasted Sweet Potato Mash

Sweet Potato Mash

1. Preheat oven to 350 F

. While oven is preheating, coat sweet potato cubes and shallot with half the butter or ghee and season with salt and pepper.

3. Roast in the oven for 30 minutes or until sweet potato is tender.

.   Remove from oven and add sweet potatoes, roasted garlic, sea salt, pepper, and the rest of the ghee to a blender and blend until smooth.

5.   Remove mixture from blender and fold in the chives.

6.   Serve immediately.

ROSEMARY & THYME SOUS VIDE NY STRIP STEAK

Using an immersion cooker, this recipe turns simple ingredients into a totally tender main course. Bag your steaks with butter and herbs, then simply cook for beef that pairs with any side dish. Stay more Bulletproof with grass-fed meat and butter, plus skip the black pepper.

Serves: 2

Sous Vide cook time: 1-2 hours

Ingredients:

- 2 NY Strip Steaks, around 1-2″ thick

- 2 Tablespoons Butter

- 2 sprigs Rosemary

- 2 sprigs Thyme

- Ground Black Pepper and Salt to Taste

Instructtions:

1. Set up Nomiku water bath and turn temp to 57°C (135°F).

. Bag the steaks with rosemary, thyme, and butter and seal using the water displacement method or using a vacuum sealer. Sous vide for 1-2 hours (1 hour per inch).

. Remove from water bath. Set a greased heavy pan or cast iron on high heat, remove steaks from bags and sear each side for 30 seconds or until a crust forms. Alternatively, use a culinary torch to brown.

4. Immediately slice and serve. It's great for brunch with eggs

5. Stay more Bulletproof with grass-fed meat and butter, plus skip the black pepper.

- <u>BACON BEEF BROCCOLI FUSION</u>

This hybrid sous vide recipe cooks beef in a water bath until tender while stir-frying fresh broccoli for a filling main dish that pairs perfectly with cauliflower rice. Keep this recipe more Bulletproof and use pastured meats, plus steam broccoli instead of stir-frying. Avoid eating garlic too often, and skip the chipotle powder if you are sensitive to nightshades.

Ingredients:

- 2 lbs beef stew meat

- 4 cloves garlic, minced
- 2 tsp Herbes de Provence
- 2 tsp salt
- 1 tsp Chipotle powder
- ½ lb bacon, chopped
- 4 cups chopped broccoli
- 2 TBSP coconut oil

Instructtions:

- In a bowl, stir together the meat, garlic, Herbes de Provence, salt and Chipotle powder.
- Add to vacuum seal bag and seal. Heat water in Sous Vide to 135 degrees.
- Add sealed bag to water and cook for at least 6 hours.
- Remove from water and set aside. Heat coconut oil in a large skillet or wok over medium-high heat.
- Add bacon and cook for about 5 minutes.
- Add broccoli and cook another 5-6 minutes, until bacon is crispy and broccoli is beginning to be tender.
- Remove broccoli and bacon from skillet.
- Add meat to skillet (leaving out the juices) and sear quickly (1-2 minutes).
- Add broccoli and bacon and stir quickly to combine.
- Remove to serving platter and enjoy! This tastes great over cauliflower rice.

SOUS VIDE STEAKS WITH GARLIC BUTTER

Cook Time: 60 minutes

Servings: 4

Ingredients:

1. Four filet mignon steaks

2. Kosher salt

3. Freshly ground pepper

4. Garlic powder

5. Two tablespoons of butter

6. One finely minced garlic clove

7. Two tablespoons of freshly chopped parsley leaves

8. One to two tablespoons of vegetable oil

Instructions:

1.   Season the steaks to taste using salt, pepper and a little amount of garlic powder.

.   Heat the water bath to the desired temperature based on the preference of doneness, from rare, medium-rare or medium and set the timer accordingly.

3.   Once the water is heated, submerge steaks in a plastic storage bag and seal.

. Prepare the garlic butter by combining softened butter with minced garlic, a pinch of salt and parsley.

5. Remove steaks from the water bath after one hour.

6. Heat two tablespoons of olive oil over high heat in a cast iron skillet

. Once the oil gets really hot, sear the steaks quickly on each side. Shouldn't take more than 1 minute per side.

8. Top the steaks with the garlic butter, allow to cool for a few minutes and serve.

Chef's tip: Garlic butter is an important ingredient of this recipe and should be prepared with the appropriate quantity of components for an excellent creamy taste.

Nutritional information

Calories: 409.8; Fats: 30.8g; Carbohydrates: 3.1g; Fiber: 0.4g; Protein: 29.7g

SEAFOOD SOUS VIDE RECIPES

- SOUS VIDE SALMON – TO BRINE OR NOT TO BRINE YOUR

Another benefit of cooking salmon (and other fish) using sous vide method is that it helps reducing that curd-like stuff that comes out of during cooking. The white stuff that is being pushed out of salmon is called albumin. America's Test Kitchen found that most of albumin is pushed out when fish is smoked, canned or poached. It has been recently discovered that brining fish can reduce the unsightly white layer of albumin that appears on the surface during cooking. Ten minutes in a one tablespoon of salt per cup of water brine is enough to minimize the effect.

The brine

The basic brine for sous vide salmon is as follows:

- 3 cups ice water
- 3 Tbsp kosher salt (sea or Himalayan salt will work great too. Himalayan salt will make the brine nicely pink as on the picture below)
- 2 Tbsp olive oil

This will be enough for a 1 1/2 lb salmon fillet. Scale proportionately if necessary.

To prepare the brine, add salt to ice water and stir until the salt is dissolved. Pour the water into a Ziploc bag, add olive oil and stir.

Brining process

- Add salmon fillets, push out as much air as possible and seal the bag. Refrigerate for about 30 minutes but no less than 10 minutes.
- You can add herbs and spices to the brine as well to add more flavor. Dill and black or white pepper are commonly added.

Preparing salmon for sous vide cooking

- Once the brining is done, remove salmon fillets from the Ziploc bag, pat dry with a paper towel and place into another (heat resistant) bag. Add a couple of tablespoons of olive oil

to prevent the fillets from sticking to each other. Gently remove as much air from the bag as possible and seal. You want to be careful not to squeeze the fillets.

_ If you have a vacuum sealer, seal the bag with a vacuum sealer on a gentle cycle. Vacuum sealing works the best. If you don't have a vacuum sealer, make sure the bag is big enough so that top end can stay out of the pot and not leak in any water.

Sous vide cooking process for salmon

There are various recommendations on what temperature is best for cooking sous vide salmon. You may find that some vary by 10 degrees or more. In the end, it all depends on personal taste. I tested several temperatures and found that Chef Steps' recommendation of cooking at 122F worked best for me. Others prefer their sous vide salmon a little more well-done and cook at higher temperatures. Just remember, 140F is the absolute maximum temperature you want to go to.

Another thing to keep in mind is the length of the cooking. The good thing about sous vide cooking is that you may cook longer than needed without any ill effect. Some people cook their sous vide salmon for an hour just to be on the safe side and ensure proper cooking. I cook my salmon for 60 minutes regardless of the size and thickness. This takes away any guesswork and makes thing simpler. As a matter of fact, Modernist Cooking Made Easy: Sous Vide: The Authoritative Guide to Low Temperature Precision Cooking recommends cooking salmon at 122F for one hour.

Cooking without an immersion circulator

Let's assume that you want to cook your salmon at 122F. Fill a large pot with hot tap water. In a typical house the hottest water out of the tap is about 123F to 128F. You want to bring the temperature to about 126F. Add cold water to bring the temperature down. Add some boiling hot water to raise the temperature. Have a pot of boiling water ready before the cooking.

The reason why you want to start at 126F is that as soon as you add a couple of cold salmon fillets, the temperature will drop to about 122F. The 126F temperature works with a medium (about a 2 gallon) pot. For a larger pot, the temperature drop will be smaller. Place the salmon inside the pot and wait for about 2 minutes to let the temperature stabilize. Stir to avoid hot/cold spots. Then check the temperature and adjust as needed. Keep checking the temperature every 7-10 minutes and adjusting as needed. Keep stirring frequently to avoid hot/cold spots.

Cooking with an immersion circulator

The preferred method is to use an immersion circulator, like the Anova Sous Vide Immersion Circulator with WiFi that I currently use. This requires an initial investment, which can be significant if you want to invest into a really good model.

Searing salmon after cooking

You will want to pan sear the salmon fillets after cooking, skin side down. This will add flavor and make the rubbery skin palatable. You don't need to sear the other side. Preheat a skillet with two tablespoons of olive oil. Sear the salmon skin down over high heat for about 45 seconds.

Remove the salmon from the pan and serve your perfectly cooked, moist and flaky sous vide salmon immediately. It will start losing the juices and drying out the longer it sits on the plate.

- SOUS VIDE SALMON

For perfect moist and flaky salmon, look no further than this sous vide recipe. Brine your filets in a saltwater and olive oil blend, then cook gently in water and garnish with fresh herbs. As long as you use wild-caught salmon and a silicone bag, this recipe stays ultra-Bulletproof.

Ingredients:

- 1 1/2 lbs salmon fillet (scaled, trimmed, cut into 4 pieces)

- 2 cups ice water

- 4 Tbsp olive oil

- 2 Tbsp kosher salt

- Fresh dill (finely chopped, for garnish)

- Fresh chives (finely chopped, for garnish)

- Lemon (cut in wedges, for garnish)

Instructions:

. To prepare the brine, add salt to ice water and stir until the salt is dissolved. Pour the water into a Ziploc bag, add olive oil and stir. You can add herbs and spices to the brine as well to add more flavor. Dill and pepper are commonly added. White pepper may be a better choice as it will be less conspicuous compared to black pepper.

. Add salmon fillets, push out as much air as possible and seal the bag. Refrigerate for about 30 minutes.

. Remove salmon from the Ziploc bag, pat dry with a paper towel and transfer into another bag. Add 1 tablespoon of olive oil to avoid the fillets sticking to each other. Gently remove as much air from the bag as possible and seal. You want to be careful not to squeeze the fish. If you have a vacuum sealer, seal the fish on a gentle cycle to preserve its shape.

. Immerse the sealed bag in preheated water and cook at 122F (or higher depending on the level of doneness you want, see the chart in the notes) for one hour, using a sous vide immersion circulator. If you don't have an immersion circulator, use the method described in the post above.

5. Shortly before the cooking is done, preheat a large skillet with 1 tablespoon of olive oil.

. Remove the salmon fillets from the bag and sear skin side down over high heat for 45 seconds. Sprinkle with chopped dill and chives. Serve immediately, with lemon wedges.

- <u>SOUS VIDE LOBSTER TAIL</u>
-

With no searing or broiling needed, this sous vide recipe produces restaurant-worthy results with simple prep. Simply shell lobster, bag with butter and parsley, and cook for 1 hour. Get wild-caught lobster and grass-fed butter for a Bulletproof take on this sous vide recipe.

Preparation time: 10 mins

Cook time: 1 hr

Ingredients:

- 2 Lobster Tails
- 10 Tbs Butter
- Fresh Parsley

TIME/TEMPERATURE

120F for 1 hour | Soft, translucent

130F for 1 hour | Tender

140F for 1-hour | Firm

Instructions:

PREPARE IT

1.   Preheat water bath to your desired temperature, based on the chart to the left.

.   Submerge frozen lobster tails in bowl of cold water for approximately 30 minutes to defrost and loosen up.

.   Cut shell down the middle with kitchen shears and slowly but firmly pull shell apart, ensuring not to rip the meat.

4.   Gently remove lobster meat from shell and de-vein, if necessary.

COOK IT

. Place lobster tails, fresh parsley, and 2-3 Tbs of butter into a heavy duty Ziploc bag. Vacuum sealing is possible, however we prefer using the water displacement method as it is less likely to deform the shape of the tail.

2.   Cook for 1 hour.

SERVE IT

. Melt 6-8 Tbs of butter in a sauce pan over medium heat. If you prefer clarified butter, heat until boiling and the butter fat separates.

2.   Serve clarified butter on plate beneath tail, or in a separate bowl.

-      <u>**SIMPLE SOUS VIDE SCALLOPS**</u>

With low mercury levels and a buttery-soft texture, scallops make the perfect candidate for Bulletproof sous vide recipes. This approach to scallops bags them with oil and spices, then gives them a quick sear after 20 minutes. Stay more Bulletproof with wild-caught seafood, plus use avocado oil or ghee for cooking and searing.

Ingredients:

- Approximately 1 lb Atlantic Sea jumbo scallops

- Salt and pepper to taste

- Olive oil

Instructions:

1. Bring the water-bath to 52C.

2. Pat dry the scallops, and sprinkle salt and fresh ground pepper generously.

3. Pace the scallops in the plastic bag, make sure to have it in single layer.

4. Drizzle olive oil into the bag.

. Make sure to remove all the air bubble from the bag when "cooking" the scallops in the water-bath. To create a vacuum in the bag, carefully place the bag with your ingredients into the water-bath, make sure to immerse the bag until near the seal, this will create a vacuum, then seal the bag.

6. Place the bags gently into the water-bath and set the time for 20 to 25 minutes.

. Once the time is up, gently remove the bag from the water-bath, drain the liquid from it and pat dry the scallops.

.   In a cast iron skillet, add a little olive oil or butter, and sear both side of the scallops until golden brown.

9.   Serve immediately.

-   <u>**SOUS VIDE SHRIMP**</u>

Frozen shrimp become perfectly tender and dippable with this sous vide recipe. Bag them with lemon and cook for 15 minutes, then dunk in ice water for an easy appetizer that will impress all your guests. To keep this recipe Bulletproof, simply use wild-caught shrimp.

Sous vide is the easiest way to perfectly cook shrimp. The shrimp are tender, sweet and juicy. Never have rubbery shrimp again.

Prep Time: 3 minutes

Cook Time: 15 minutes

Additional Time: 30 minutes

Total Time: 48 minutes

Ingredients:

•   1 lb Shrimp, Deveined, Shells On

•   3 Slices Lemon

•   2 Bay Leaves

Instructtions:

1. Cooking shrimp is super easy and goes from raw to done in the blink of an eye. Once it crosses over to well done, there is no going back. You have chewy, rubbery shrimp. Not good.
2. Using the sous vide to cook your shrimp at a specific temperature you are ensuring that the shrimp will not get over cooked.

Best Way To Poach Shrimp:

- Preheat your Sous Vide to 135 °F / 57 °C

  If you are using a metal pot, be sure to put a hot pad under the stockpot to protect your surface.

- Make sure there is enough water for all the shrimp to be submerged by a few inches.

Shrimp:

These are 26-30 shrimp. That means in terms of size there are twenty six to thirty shrimp per pound. The higher the number, the smaller the shrimp.

- These shrimp are frozen and they should be thawed under cold running water.

  These shrimp are deveined but still have their tails and shells on. The tails and shells give great flavor so I wait until after they are cooked to remove them. You are welcome to remove the shells before you sous vide them.

- Add about 3 slices of lemon and a bay leaf or two to the shrimp.

Clamp:

- Remove as much air as possible and flatten out the shrimp so it is in an even layer.

- If you have a vacuum sealer, set the vacuum to moist and remove the air and seal.

- Make sure that the shrimp are completely submerged in the water.

Cook;

- Cook for 15 minutes.

- The shrimp are now pretty close to perfect!

Normally with sous vide you have a window of time to remove the food from the water. With shrimp that window is about 15 minutes.

Cook your shrimp for 15 minutes and remove them from the water bath within 15 minutes. If you totally forget, don't panic. You should be good to go for up to an hour after the cooking time. But don't go over an hour and remove it as soon as possible.

Ice Bath:

- Remove the perfectly cooked shrimp and plunge them in an ice bath.

This will stop the cooking process and drop the temperature to ensure they are in a safe temperature zone for storage.

Easy Poached Shrimp:

Peel the shrimp leaving the tails in place and you are all set to make a sous vide shrimp cocktail!

SOUS VIDE RECIPES: CHICKEN, LAMB, & PORK

- ## SOUS VIDE STEAK WITH PONZU SAUCE

Cook Time: 1 hour 10 minutes

Servings: 2

Ingredients:

1. Two beef steaks which should be at least 1 inch thick

2. Four tablespoons of neutral frying oil

3. Two tablespoons of unsalted butter

4. Sea Salt to taste

5. Fresh cilantro leaves to garnish (optional)

Ponzu sauce

6. Two teaspoons of lemon juice

7. One teaspoon of orange juice

8. One tablespoon of rice vinegar

9. One tablespoon of Japanese sake

10. One teaspoon of soy sauce

11. Digital thermometer with an oven-safe probe

Instructions:

- Arrange the steaks on a baking tray of small size and put inside the freezer. Leave for about 30 minutes, so that the exterior can freeze.

- Preheat your oven to 158oF or the lowest temperature on your oven and place a baking rack over a baking tray.

- Heat a heavy skillet over medium-high heat until it's hot; while preheating the skillet, brush both sides of the steaks with oil.

- Brown the steaks one at a time, 30 seconds per side, until all the steaks have both of their surfaces turned dark brown. Then transfer the steaks instantly onto the prepared baking rack.

- Insert the oven-safe probe of the digital thermometer from the side, into the thickest part of the thinnest steak. Set the alarm to the temperature of your choosing.

- Bake until the steak reaches the set temperature; baking time for proper cooking is determined by your oven and the thickness of the steak.

- Combine all the ingredients for the ponzu sauce in a small bowl for proper mixing and then set aside.

- Once the steak is out of the oven, brush with melted butter and season generously using sea salt.

- Cut the steak into chewable sized pieces and serve immediately with cilantro leaves as garnish and the ponzu sauce for dipping.

Chef's tip: Do not use a nonstick skillet for this as the high heat will damage the coating and only judge the doneness of the steak by its core temperature.

Nutritional information

Calories: 188; Fats: 6.2g; Carbohydrates: 7.1g; Fiber: 0.3g; Protein: 25.1g

- <u>SOUS VIDE CHICKEN PICCATA</u>

Cook time: 4 hours 15 minutes

Servings: 5

Ingredients:

1. 1 lb. of boneless breast

2. One cup of chicken stock

3. Two tablespoons of All-purpose flour

4. Half a cup of extra virgin olive oil

5. A quarter cup of sun-dried tomatoes in oil, which should be chopped

6. One tablespoon of chopped capers

7. One can of quartered artichoke hearts, which should be drained and well-rinsed

8. Three minced garlic cloves

9. Half a cup of dry white wine

10. A quarter cup of butter, which should be divided into four pieces

11. A quarter cup of chopped fresh parsley

12. Kosher salt

13. Freshly ground black pepper

14. Zest and juice from one lemon

Instructions:

The chicken:

.   Season the chicken with salt and pepper; put in a vacuum seal bag, seal and put in the water bath.

2.   Cook for four hours at 66°C and afterward, remove from the water bath and set aside.

The sauce:

.   Heat olive oil in a large deep skillet over medium-high heat; add flour and whisk for about one minute until slightly browned.

.   Add garlic and sun-dried tomatoes, and continue whisking for another 30 seconds to one minute. Gradually add chicken stock while whisking.

.   Add capers, artichoke hearts, wine as well as lemon zest and juice. At the same time, carefully add chicken cooking liquid from the bag.

. Continue cooking over medium-high heat until the mixture becomes slightly reduced and thickened; shouldn't take more than seven minutes max.

7.   As the mixture is reducing, cut the chicken into slices.

.   Once there is a reduction in the sauce mixture, remove from heat; add the butter pats and stir;

. Add chicken and parsley; use salt and pepper to season to your taste; serve instantly with either potatoes or pasta.

Chef's tip: Ensure that the sauce is thickened before putting in the chicken and parsley.

Nutritional information

Calories: 520.2; Fats: 12.3g; Carbohydrates: 47.8g; Fiber: 2.9g; Protein: 47.1g

- ## SOUS VIDE CHIMICHURRI LAMB CHOPS

Cook time: 2 hours

Servings: 6

Ingredients:

Lamb Chops

1. Two racks of lamb, which should be frenched

2. Two crushed garlic cloves

3. Salt and pepper

Basil Chimichurri

4. One cup of finely chopped fresh basil

5. One diced shallot

6. One to two clove (s) of minced garlic, minced

7. One teaspoon of red chili flakes

8. Half tablespoon of olive oil

9. Three tablespoons of red wine vinegar

10. A quarter teaspoon of sea salt

11. A quarter teaspoon of pepper

Instructions:

1.   Set the sous vide temperature to 133oF.

2.   Season the lamb generously using salt and pepper.

.   Put in a bag and vacuum-seal along with crushed garlic after which you can then sous vide for two hours.

.   Get a bowl, combine all the ingredients of the basil chimichurri sauce in it and mix adequately.

5.   Season to taste, cover up and refrigerate so that the flavors can blend together.

6.   After two hours, remove the lamb chops from the bag and dry well with paper towel.

.   Sear with a scalding hot well-oiled pan. Cut into slices between the bones and top liberally with basil chimichurri sauce before serving.

Chef's tip: The ingredients should be well combined so as to enjoy the excellent combination of flavors that this meal provides.

Nutritional information

Calories: 25; Fats: 0g; Carbohydrates: 6g; Fiber: 1.5g; Protein: 0.5g

INDIAN-STYLE SOUS VIDE CHICKEN THIGHS AND CREAMED SPINACH OVER CAULIFLOWER MASH

This all-in-one sous vide recipe combines tender chicken thighs with a creamy spinach and cauliflower sides, all mixed with warm flavors from curry powder and turmeric. Stay more Bulletproof and use pastured chicken, steam spinach separately before adding to the recipe, and avoid eating garlic too often.

Ingredients:

- 4 boneless, skinless chicken thighs

- 1 head of cauliflower

- 1 large bag of spinach

- 1 can of coconut full-fat coconut milk

- 1 T yellow curry powder

- 1 T paprika

- 1 T tumeric

- 1 T cumin

- 1/2 T powdered garlic

- Salt and Pepper to taste

- A couple dashes of cayenne for some extra heat (optional)

- Ghee, butter or your favorite cooking oil

- Green onions - for garnish

Instructions:

- Mix the spices together into a spice blend. –

- Prepare your Gramercy Kitchen Co. sous vide set up.

  Program your device to run at 165F for 1-2 hours. Any time within this range will work, depending on how much time you happen to have.

  Salt the chicken thighs fairly generously - this helps the flavor to penetrate the chicken thighs as they cook. Then, cover your chicken thighs in half the spice blend.

  Place the seasoned chicken thighs into your sous vide bags and add a healthy glug of your cooking oil. Then seal using your preferred method. Massage the bag in your hand to ensure the oil has evenly coated the chicken thighs.

  Once your Gramercy Kitchen Co. sous vide set up has come to temp, place the bag of chicken thighs in the water and let run.

- When about 20 minutes remains on the cook time, get ready to finish the meal off.

  Heat a large skillet to medium high heat. Place the spinach along with the coconut milk in the pan. Add the remainder of the spice blend. Let simmer on medium-high heat while stirring constantly as the spinach wilts.

  While the spinach cooks, chop up ahead of cauliflower and blend until fairly smooth in a blender with powdered garlic, salt and pepper to taste. Transfer the mixture into a pan on the stove at medium and heat through. Add some a lump of ghee or a pat of butter for some additional flavor and creaminess.

Once your GKC sous vide unit beeps, it's time to bring it all together. Cut open your bag, and using a pair of thongs, remove your chicken from the bag and place on a cutting board. Chop into strips.

On a plate, place your cauliflower mash and creamed spinach side by side. Place a chopped chicken thigh on top of the cauliflower mash and top with green onion.

- ## <u>SOUS VIDE WHOLE CHICKEN</u>

Try a whole new take on roast chicken with this sous vide recipe. Bag your bird with a spice rub, cook in a water bath, then sear on all sides for a totally tender main dish. Keep it more Bulletproof with grass-fed butter, avoid the dried pepper if you are sensitive to nightshades, and swap garlic with lemon or your favorite fresh herbs.

Ingredients:

- 1 whole chicken (4-5 pounds)
- 2 tablespoons unsalted butter
- Fresh cilantro for serving

For the chicken dry rub:

- 2 teaspoons Kosher salt
- 2 teaspoons paprika

- 1 teaspoon cayenne pepper

- 1 teaspoon dried thyme

- 2 teaspoons ground black pepper

- 1/2 teaspoon garlic powder

Instructions:

1. Preheat water to 150°F using a sous vide precision cooker (I use Anova sous vide).

2. Prepare chicken by rinsing under cold water. Pat dry with paper towels and set it aside.

. Mix the dry rub ingredients on a big plate. Now, prepare a large sous vide bag or a Ziploc bag by folding the top of the bag back over itself to form a hem. This will prevent chicken seasonings from getting on the edges of the bag. Set aside.

. Place the chicken on the plate and rub the mixture all over it. Sprinkle the excess dry rub inside the chicken if there's any left.

. Slide the chicken into the prepared bag. Unfold the edge before closing the bag. Seal the bag using either a vacuum sealer or a hand pump.

. Lower your bagged chicken into the preheated water bath, making sure the whole chicken is under the waterline. If using Ziploc bag, slowly lower your bagged chicken into your water bath, letting the pressure of the water press air out through the top of the bag. Once most of the air is out of the bag, carefully seal the bag just above the waterline. Cook for 6 hours.

. Once the chicken is done, remove from the water bath and transfer it onto a plate. Gently pat with paper towels. Preserve the cooking liquid from the bag if you like for serving or for flavorful chicken soup or chicken stock later.

. Heat a cast iron skillet over high heat. Melt butter and sear the whole chicken on all sides until the skin is golden brown and crispy, about 5 minutes. You can also cut up the chicken first before searing.

9. Serve with fresh cilantro. Enjoy!

- SOUS VIDE LAMB CHOPS

Sous vide cooking creates ultra-juicy lamb chops, and this recipe ensures the perfect cooking temp and time. Submerge your chops with herbs and butter, then sear when they become perfectly tender. Keep it all more Bulletproof and use grass-fed butter and lamb, plus skip the pepper and garlic.

Ingredients:

- 4 lamb chops
- 2 garlic cloves
- 1 teaspoon fresh rosemary
- 1 teaspoon fresh thyme
- Salt and pepper

- 1 tablespoon butter (optional as the meat doesn't really need it)

Instructions:

1. Preheat the sous vide to 140 degrees F.

, Salt and pepper the lamb chops, sprinkle them with rosemary and thyme and lay sliced garlic on each of the chops.

3. Add in a tablespoon of butter and place the seasoned chops into a bag.

4. Seal the bag and immerse in the sous vide.

5. Cook for about an hour per inch of lamb chop thickness,

6. I cooked mine for about 2 1/2 hours.

7. Once they are done sear quickly on high heat just to brown them and serve.

SOUS VIDE PORK CHOPS

Using this sous vide recipe, you'll never have to eat a dry and chewy pork chop again. Season bone-in chops, then bag with herbs and lemon before searing with wholesome cooking fats. For a more Bulletproof chop, skip the pepper, get pastured pork, and sear in pastured lard, ghee, or coconut oil.

Serves: 1

Ingredients:

- 1 bone-in pork chop, about ¾ inch thick

- ¾ teaspoon fine grain sea salt

- ¼ teaspoon fresh ground pepper

- 1 sprig fresh rosemary

- 1 slice lemon

- ½ tablespoon lard, bacon fat or coconut oil

OPTIONAL SERVING:

- Sauerkraut

Instructions:

. Season pork chop on all sides with salt and pepper. Place in sous vide bag and add the rosemary and lemon. Seal bags closed to make sure no air pockets remain in the bag.

. Use the Joule app on your phone and select Pork Chop. Select your desired doneness (I chose 140 degrees which was recommended on the Joule app) and place filled bag in water bath. Allow to come to temp for about 45 minutes. It will hold it at the perfect temp for an additional 90 minutes so don't worry if you are not home when it is finished.

. Heat cast iron skillet with ½ tablespoon lard to medium high heat. Remove chop from bag and place into the hot oil. Sear on both sides until golden brown and a crust forms, about 1-minute per side. Remove from heat and serve over sauerkraut.

Nutritional Info:

279 calories, 19g fat, 24g protein, 1g carbs, 0.4g fiber

SOUS VIDE GARLIC CILANTRO CHICKEN

While this sous vide recipe marinates your chicken in a homemade cilantro dressing, you can use any marinade you fancy. Using a spatchcock cut, chicken cooks evenly and gets evenly coated in your marinade mix before broiling for a few minutes to finish. Stay Bulletproof on this one with a pastured bird, swap olive oil with avocado oil or ghee, and avoid eating garlic and pepper too often.

Prep Time: 8 hours

Cook Time: 4 hours

Total Time: 19 hours

Course: Main Dish

Servings: 4 people

Ingredients:

- 1 Whole Chicken

- 1 Head garlic peeled

- 1 Big Bunch Cilantro

- 1 Tablespoon Black Peppercorns

- 1/2 Cup olive oil

- Salt to taste

Instructions:

1.   Puree the garlic, cilantro, black peppercorns, and olive oil in a food processor.

2.   Put the chicken and cilantro puree in a sous vide bag and marinate in the chiller overnight.

3.   Cook the chicken for 4 hours at 150F.

4.   Transfer the chicken to an ice bath.

5.   Get the chicken out of the bag and broil for 15 minutes at 425F.

1. BARBECUE SHORT RIBS

Cook time: 72 hours

Servings: 3

Ingredients:

1. Three-quarter cup of unsweetened pineapple juice

2. Half a cup of peanut oil

3. One-third cup of soy sauce

4. A quarter cup of molasses

5. One teaspoon of ground ginger

6. One pound of short ribs

7. One teaspoon each of Kosher salt and freshly ground black pepper to taste

Instructions:

Barbecue Sauce:

1. Combine the first five ingredients in a bowl for proper mixing

. In another bowl, pour the already prepared sauce over the short ribs and then cover to refrigerate overnight.

3. Preheat your water bath to 54oC.

4. Vacuum seal the ribs with the sauce on it.

5. Place into the water bath and cook for seventy-two hours.

Chef's tip: Patience is required here as it takes three days for it to be ready; so, don't be in a hurry.

Nutritional information

Calories: 300; Fats: 23g; Carbohydrates: 7g; Fiber: 0g; Protein: 17g

- **<u>CAJUN-SEASONED TILAPIA</u>**

Cook Time: 30 minutes

Servings: 1

Ingredients:

1. Two tilapia fillets

2. A quarter cup of Cajun seasoning

3. Two tablespoons of garlic powder

4. Two tablespoons of dried onion granules

5. Two tablespoons of Italian seasoning

6. Two tablespoons of cayenne pepper

7. One tablespoon of black pepper

8. One tablespoon of kosher salt

9. One tablespoon of smoked paprika

Instructions:

1.   Preheat sous vide water bath to 57°C.

.   Prepare the Cajun seasoning by combining the last seven ingredients together in a container and then set aside.

3.   Pat the tilapia dry and use Cajun seasoning generously on both sides.

4.   Arrange the tilapia fillets into a Ziploc bag or Vacuum sealing bag and seal. Seal.

.   Submerge the bag in the water bath and cook for thirty minutes. After cooking, remove the tilapia from the bag, pat dry and sear.

It can be served with vegetables, seasoned rice or remoulade sauce.

Chef's tip: Do not allow the tilapia fillets to overlap so as to enable proper cooking.

Nutritional information

Calories: 143.9; Fats: 6.3g; Carbohydrates: 0g; Fiber: 0g; Protein: 21g

- MAPLE ROASTED BUTTERNUT SQUASH

Cook time: 1hour

Servings: 6

Ingredients:

1. One butternut squash (To be peeled and cut into chunky pieces)

2. One tablespoon of maple syrup

3. One teaspoon of chopped fresh thyme

4. Half teaspoon of garlic powder

5. One teaspoon of chopped pancetta (optional)

6. Salt and pepper

7. Two tablespoons of toasted pumpkin seeds (to be used for garnishing)

Instructions:

1. Set your water bath or circulator to 172°F

. Put all the contents except for the pumpkin seeds in a Ziploc bag, shake well, remove the air from the bag and seal it up after which you can cook for forty-five minutes to one hour.

.   Remove the contents from the pouch and place on a dry towel to extract the liquid and set it aside to be used later.

.   Heat the squash over high heat in a pan until it turns golden, add the earlier extracted liquid and glaze.

5.   Serve alongside the chopped pancetta and toasted pumpkin seeds.

Chef's tip: To get a more pleasant taste, add some feta cheese and fresh tomatoes.

Nutritional information

Calories: 207.4; Fats: 10.3g; Carbohydrates: 30.5g; Fiber: 4.8g; Protein: 1.5g

VEGGIE SOUS VIDE RECIPES

- <u>HONEY GLAZED SOUS VIDE RAINBOW CARROTS</u>

Tough root vegetables become totally tender with sous vide cooking — and this recipe upgrades an already sweet veggie with a buttery honey glaze. To stay more Bulletproof, use grass-fed butter and raw honey.

Ingredients:

- For the Sous Vide Rainbow Carrots
- 8 to 12 rainbow carrots, peeled and cut into 3" sticks (76mm)
- 2 tablespoons butter (30ml)
- 2 teaspoons honey (10ml)
- To Assemble
- 1 lemon
- Honey
- Coarse sea salt

Instructions:

1. Preheat the water bath to 183°F (83.9°C).

. Combine all ingredients into a sous vide bag, trying to keep the thickness of the bag less than 1" (25mm) for even cooking, and seal.

3. Place the bag in the water bath and cook for 45 to 60 minutes, until tender.

- <u>SOUS VIDE CARROT AND SWEET POTATO MASH</u>

This smooth and starchy mash gets natural sweetness from the veggies themselves, while sous vide cooking makes an ultra-tender base without babysitting your stove top. With four simple ingredients and an hour of cook time, sous vide recipes can't get any simpler. Keep it more Bulletproof and use grass-fed butter.

Ingredients:

* 4 large 1 inchs carrots , cut into long pieces

* 2 large 1 sweet potatoes " , peeled and cut into slices

* 1 tbsp butter

* To taste Salt

Instructions:

1. Heat the sous vide bath to 183F.

. Vacuum seal the carrots and sweet potatoes into separate bags. If you don't have a vacuum sealer, you can use a ziploc bag with the water displacement method. Due to the odd size of the vegetables, you'll surely have air in the bags regardless of the method you use.

. Put both bags of veggies into the sous vide bath, and weigh them down with a pot lid, kitchen utensil or anything else that will keep the bags fully submerged.

4.   Cook at 183F for at least 1 hour.

.   Pull both bags out of the bath. Dump the veggies into a large bowl and add the butter and a dash of salt.

. Mash the heck out of them until you have a consistency you like with either a standard potato masher or, my favorite, an immersion blender.

RECIPE NOTES

If you aren't eating right away, after pulling the bags out of the sous vide bath, you can put them in the refrigerator for up to a week. When you're ready to eat, heat them back up in a sous vide bath at least 130F, but no hotter than 183F.

-   SOUS VIDE ASPARAGUS WITH MINT

With a stiff texture in its raw state, asparagus is made for sous vide recipes. In just 15 minutes, this recipe creates perfectly crisp stalks, all drenched in a simple buttery mint sauce. To stay more Bulletproof, simply use grass-fed butter.

This recipe makes about 2-4 servings, depending on how large your asparagus bunch is and how much everyone loves asparagus. Once you've made asparagus in a Sous Vide you'll never want it any other way.

Ingredients (Sous Vide Asparagus):

- Bunch asparagus (break at stalk)
- 3 tablespoons unsalted butter, cut into 3-4 pieces
- Sea salt
- Fresh mint leaves, sliced in chiffonade

Instructions (Sous Vide Asparagus):

1. Set the temperature of your Sous Vide Cooker to 185°F (85°C).

. Place asparagus in a vacuum seal bag. Add the butter and a pinch of salt. Seal the bag using a vacuum sealer on the dry setting.

. Place the bag in the preheated water bath and set a timer for 10 to 12 minutes, depending on the thickness of the asparagus.

. Remove the bag from the water bath when your timer goes off. Carefully open the bag and remove the asparagus spears, arrange on a serving plate. Spoon some of the butter from the bag over the spears. Garnish with sea salt and mint leaves.

.

- ## HEALTHY SOUS VIDE GARLIC MASHED CAULIFLOWER

Sous vide makes this creamy low-carb side dish even more simple and delicious. Florets gently cook in a water bath with butter and spices, then blend into creamy perfection. To stay more Bulletproof, it's best to enjoy your cauliflower steamed or boiled with the cooking water drained — plus, use grass-fed butter, swap olive oil with avocado oil, and avoid eating garlic too often.

Mashed cauliflower is a great way to up your healthy vegetables and adhere to a variety of diets including keto, low carb, Whole 30, Atkins, vegetarian and vegan diets. The best news is this cauliflower mash is thoroughly delicious, feels extravagant, can be varied in multiple ways and is super easy to make.

Cook: 1 hour

Total: 1 hour, 10 mins

Yield: 4 Servings

Ingredients:

- 1 medium head cauliflower or 2 pounds bagged cauliflower florets or riced cauliflower

- 2 T butter

- Kosher salt and pepper to taste

- 1/4 t cayenne pepper

- 1 - 2 heads fresh garlic

- 1 T olive oil

- 1/3 to 1/2 cup chicken stock, vegetable stock, cream or water

Instructions:

. Heat your sous vide bath to 190 degrees. You can shorten the preheating by starting with hot water from the tap. Heat your oven to 400 degrees.

. Remove the cauliflower leaves and slice into 1/2" slices. Chop the slices into 1/2" pieces. Place the cauliflower in a 1 gallon Ziploc freezer bag with the butter and seasoning. Vacuum seal the bag by using the air displacement method. Alternatively, use a vacuum seal machine to remove the air and seal the bag.

3. Add the bag to the 190 degree sous vide bath and cook for one hour.

. While the cauliflower is in the sous vide, prepare and roast your garlic. Slice off about 3/4" off the pointy top of a head of garlic. Drizzle a little olive oil over the cut, replace the portion you cut off and wrap the entire head in tin foil. Roast in the oven for 40-50 minutes until the garlic is soft. Remove and set aside.

. If making the cauliflower mash for a later time, remove the cauliflower bag from the bath and plunge it into a bowl of ice water for 10 minutes before transferring to the fridge. The sous vide cauliflower will last for 5 days in the fridge or longer in the freezer. When ready to finish the cauliflower mash you can return it to a 150-degree sous vide for 20 to 30 minutes.

. If preparing the cauliflower mash directly from the sous vide dump the contents into a blender or food processor. Squeeze out the soft roasted garlic into the blender and add 1/4 cup of a liquid of your choice: stock, cream or water. Blend until smooth adding more liquid if needed. Taste and adjust seasonings

SOUS VIDE CARROTS

Cook **time:** 25 minutes

Serving: 1

Ingredients:

1. Baby carrots

2. Olive oil

3. Pinch of salt

4. Knob of butter

5. One tablespoon of honey

Instructions:

1. Preheat the water bath to 185oF

. Arrange a single layer of baby carrots in a vacuum bag and add some quantity of olive oil along with a pinch of salt, honey, and cardamom.

3. Vacuum seal the bag and place it in the water bath to cook for twenty-five minutes

. Remove the carrots from the bag and pat dry to remove the liquid. Serve immediately with a knob of butter

Chef's tip: Increasing the number or size of the carrots doesn't affect the cooking time or temperature.

Nutritional information

Calories: 25; Fats: 0g; Carbohydrates: 6g; Fiber: 1.5g; Protein: 0.5g

- <u>SOUS VIDE MUSHROOMS</u>

Cook time: 30 minutes

Servings: 4

Ingredients:

1. 1 lb. of assorted mushrooms which should be cleaned, rinsed and cut into bite-size pieces

2. Two tablespoons of low sodium soy sauce

3. Two tablespoons of extra-virgin olive oil

4. One tablespoon of sherry vinegar or white vinegar

5. Two teaspoons of fresh thyme leaves

6. Half teaspoon of freshly ground black pepper

7. Half teaspoon of kosher salt plus more to taste

Instructions:

1.   Preheat your water bath to 176°F.

2.   Combine the mushrooms with the rest of the ingredients in a bowl and toss for even coating.

3.   Place the mushroom mixture in the bag and seal.

4.   Lower the bagged mushrooms into the water bath and cook for thirty minutes.

5.   Afterward, remove the bag from the water bath and serve the mushrooms.

Chef's tip: Toss all the ingredients together for proper distribution and equal coating.

Nutritional information

Calories: 22; Fats: 0.3g; Carbohydrates: 3.3g; Fiber: 1g; Protein: 3.1g

SOUS VIDE MASHED POTATOES

Cook time: 2 hours and 25 minutes

Servings: 5

Ingredients:

1. Two pounds of Russet potatoes

2. Five cloves of garlic

3. Three rosemary sprigs

4. Eight ounces of unsalted butter

5. One cup of whole milk

6. Two teaspoons of kosher salt

Instructions:

1.   Preheat your sous vide water bath to 90oC.

2.   Rinse and peel the potatoes, then slice them thinly into 1/8-inch pieces.

3.   Smash and peel the cloves of garlic.

. Put the potatoes, garlic, rosemary, butter, milk, and salt into a zip or vacuum seal bag for sealing and cook until the potatoes are tender, should not take more than 11/2 hours.

.   Open the bag and extract the liquid through a sieve into a small bowl and set aside. Discard whatever is left.

6.   Put the potatoes in a large bowl and get them mashed.

. Gently whisk the melted butter and milk (that had been previously set aside) back into the mashed potatoes to obtain a smooth and creamy texture.

Chef's tip: Use a potato ricer or food mill rather than a food processor or mixer so that you don't end up with a potato that has a gluey texture.

Nutritional information

Calories: 88; Fats: 2.8g; Carbohydrates: 15g; Fiber: 1.3g; Protein: 1.7g

- **GRILLED BRUSSELS SPROUTS**

Cook Time: 1 hour, 15 minutes

Servings: 4

Ingredients:

1. One pound of brussels sprouts

2. One tablespoon of olive oil

3. Two garlic cloves, which should be smashed and minced

4. A pinch of salt

5. Freshly ground pepper

6. Bamboo skewers.

Instructions:

1.   Preheat the sous vide water bath to 82oC.

2.   Clean and trim the sprouts.

3.   Combine the oil, garlic, salt, and pepper together in a small bowl for

proper mixing.

4.   Put the trimmed sprouts in a sous vide bag and then add the olive oil-garlic mixture.

5.   Seal the bag and submerge in the water bath setting the timer for one hour.

6.   Once it's done, remove the sprouts and allow to cool.

.   Heat your grill to medium heat and thread the sprouts on bamboo skewers which have been soaked in water for a minimum of ten minutes.

.   Place the sprouts on the heated grill and let each side be grilled for about 2 or 3 minutes after which you can serve.

Chef's tip: Ensure that the sprouts are really tender before placing them on the grill to achieve excellent results.

Nutritional information

Calories: 56; Fats: 0.8g; Carbohydrates: 11g; Fiber: 4.1g; Protein: 4g

-    **SOUS VIDE TOMATO SAUCE**

Cook Time: 58 minutes

Servings: 2

Ingredients:

1. Two tablespoons olive oil

2. Half a cup of chopped shallot

3. Half a cup of chopped onion

4. Two sliced garlic cloves

5. Three sprigs of fresh oregano

6. Two pounds of ripe tomatoes

7. Three sprigs of fresh whole thyme

8. Six large basil leaves, which should be chopped

9. One-third cup of chopped parsley leaves

Instructions:

1.   Preheat your sous vide water bath to 181oF.

. Sauté the onion, shallot, garlic, and oregano in the olive oil for 5 to 7 minutes over medium heat.

. Put the tomatoes in a Ziploc bag along with the herbs, sautéed vegetable mix, salt, and pepper. Ensure to remove the air before closing up the bag and putting it in the water bath; then cook for 50 minutes.

4.   Afterward, remove the bag from the water, and allow it to cool for a few minutes.

.   Peel the tomatoes; by now, the skin should come off very easily after cooking. Bring out the thyme stems and dispose of them.

.   Combine the peeled tomatoes and the remaining contents of the bag in a food processor and pulse until desired texture is achieved.

Chef's tip: Do not sauté the veggies beyond the recommended time.

Nutritional information

Calories: 29; Fats: 0.2g; Carbohydrates: 7g; Fiber: 1.5g; Protein: 1.3g

SOUS VIDE RECIPES: DESSERTS

- ### <u>SOUS VIDE FLOURLESS CHOCOLATE CAKE</u>

Yes, you can make dessert sous vide recipes! This take on cake blends rich ingredients like eggs, chocolate, and butter, then cooks them gently in a mason jar — so delicious, your guests won't believe you cooked it in water. To keep it Bulletproof, skip the liqueur, use grass-fed butter, and get a high-quality chocolate with at least 85% cacao.

Ingredients (For 6):

•   4 large eggs, cold

•   ½ pound semisweet chocolate (chips or squares, chopped) bittersweet may also be used

•   4 ounces butter

OPTIONAL INGREDIENTS

•   1/8 cup coffee liqueur or orange liqueur

•   2 tbsp unsweetened cocoa for dusting the cakes

Instructions:

-      Prepare your water bath, set the Anova Sous Vide Precision Cooker to 115°F / 46.1°C. Place chocolate, butter and coffee or liqueur if using, in a ziplock freezer bag and place in the water bath for 15 minutes to melt chocolate. Agitate or massage the bag every 5 minutes to ensure the mixture is well blended.

- Remove the bag and set the Anova Sous Vide Precision Cooker to 170°F / 76.7°C.

- Prepare six 4oz (125ml) mason jars by spraying the inside liberally with non stick spray or grease with butter.

- Beat the eggs in the bowl of a standing mixer at high speed until the volume doubles.

- Turn the mixer on low, cut the corner off the freezer bag and drizzle the melted chocolate mixture in slowly until the mixture is totally homogeneous.

- Scrape the batter into the prepared canning jars and smooth the surface by tapping the jar firmly but gently on the palm of your hand.

- Screw the canning jar lids on FINGER TIGHT ONLY. Place jars carefully into your water bath for 60 minutes.

Finishing Steps

- Remove jars carefully from the hot water bath and set on a wire rack; cool to room temperature. Cover and refrigerate at least 6 hours. (The cakes can be covered and refrigerated for up to 10 days.) If you peek you may find the cake looks not quite set while it is warm, it will firm up as it cools.

- About 30 minutes before serving, run a thin knife around the edge of the cakes (they may just slip out of the cup on their own.) You may garnish with berries, cream, or sieve a light sprinkling of unsweetened cocoa over the cake to decorate.

- <u>LUSCIOUS PALEO LEMON CURD</u>

You'll want to enjoy this silky-smooth curd on everything from paleo pancakes to sugar cookies, and this sous vide recipe makes it easy to prepare. Blend ingredients like lemons, raw honey, and eggs in a food processor before gently cooking for 40 minutes — no need for frequent stirring. Stay more Bulletproof with grass-fed ghee or butter in this recipe.

Prep Time: 10 mins

Cook Time: 40 mins

Total Time: 50 mins

Yield: 2-3 cups

Ingredients:

- 3 Meyer lemons, zested then juiced
- 1/2 cup raw honey
- 1/3 cup ghee or butter, melted
- 4 eggs
- 1/2 cup lemon juice (from the 3 lemons)
- 1 inch fresh ginger, grated on microplane
- Pinch of sea salt

Instructions:

1. Zest lemons using microplane or vegetable peeler (make sure to avoid white pith.)

. In a food processor, add zest, honey and grated ginger, pulsing first then process until zest is combined.

3. Next, add melted ghee/butter and process.

4. Then add in eggs, one at a time until combined.

5. Finally, add lemon juice and sea salt and process until just mixed.

. Fill sterilized canning jars with lemon curd and place lid on. Submerge in water bath and cook at 79* C for 40 minutes (-OR- pour lemon curd into a stock pot and cook over low heat for approx 10 minutes stirring frequently)

7. Gently whisk the curd to stir and then reseal jars.

. Cool jars in an immersion ice water bath set at 0*C for about 20 minutes or until chilled (-OR- put jars in refrigerator to cool)

9. Enjoy!

- <u>SOUS VIDE STRAWBERRIES</u>

This one-ingredient sous vide recipe elevates the natural sweetness in strawberries and turns them into a luxurious, succulent garnish. Bag berries and cook for 20 minutes for the perfect dessert all on its own, or a mouthwatering topping for vanilla ice cream. To stay even more Bulletproof, use fresh, organic strawberries.

Prep Time: 5m

Cook Time: 19m

Total Time: 25m

Serves: 2 people

Category: Fruit

Ingredients:

-   500 grams fresh British strawberries

Instructions:

1.   Set the water bath to 80°C

.   Place the strawberries into a vacuum sealer bag (you may need two) and seal using the Clifton at Home tabletop vacuum sealer.

3.   Put the strawberries into the Clifton at Home water bath and leave to cook for 20 minutes.

4.   Once cooked, take out of the water bath and place in a bowl.

.   You can use this for a number of desserts including trifle, cheesecake and of course our Clifton at Home Apple and Strawberry Crumble!

CONCLUSION

Sous vide cooking is taking the world by storm. People are finding that they can cook delicious meals without burning or overcooking their meat in the process. The one item we recommend to everyone that has a sous vide is to buy this Sous Vide Cookbook.

Sous vide cooking is a technique of cooking that has to do with cooking in a water bath in which the temperature is accurately regulated or controlled. Also, it involves using vacuum-sealed bags or Ziploc bags which are the appropriate materials used for cooking the ingredients. One major advantage of Sous vide cooking technique is that it provides unrivaled control over the food being cooked irrespective of the type or category of food. You are guaranteed to get excellent results just about every time you apply this technique.